Financial Jokes for Financial Folks

Andrew D. Worden

ISBN: 9781689761666

DEDICATION

I dedicate this book to my fiancé, Emily, for writing one of these jokes (I won't tell you which one) and being the best thing that's ever happened to me.

Additionally, I dedicate this book to everyone in my accounting department. Without you guys these jokes would be even worse.

And most importantly, I'd like to dedicate this book to our cat, Captain PicklePaws, for his unwavering support. Just kidding. He's a cat. He bit me the other day.

What am I supposed to put here? I'm using one of those book template things and this page is just blank. Hmmm… maybe I can put in a plug for my website. Hey! Check out my website:

www.funnymanfinance.com

I add new jokes (almost) every week. You'll be disappointed.

CONTENTS

(Jokes on you)

(There's no pages numbers)

What kind of debt did the secret agent issue?

A bond, James Bond.

Why can't the car payment make any friends?

Because they're always "a loan"

Why was the accountant sitting on her front porch?

She was waiting for her tax to return

Why do fixed interest rates smell so bad?

Because they never change

I keep trying to tell my accounting jokes at work…

But my boss says it's hardly "material"

What does an accountant use to hang decorations?

Tax

What did the financially responsible student do to get good grades?

They paid off their "principal"

What do you call really tall expenses?

Overhead

What happens when you bite quarters and nickels?

They turn into bit-coin

How did the Medical Plan say goodbye?

Deductible waived

Why did the accountant push the salaries, wages, and bonuses down the hill?

She wanted to see the payroll

How did the accountant unlock their door?

They used their ten key

Why did the financial analyst give his daughter gifts today instead of waiting until Christmas?

Because he understands "Present Value"

Did you hear about the new superhero, Accounts Payable Woman?

She had superhuman li-abilities

Why did the Accounting Department host an awards show?

To give the revenue recognition

How does a good-looking man get paid?

Handsomely

What do you call a mean bill that hasn't been paid yet?

"Accrued" Expense

Did you hear that a couple of accountants made a music album?

It was produced by Financial Records

Why did the investor think he could sell his lakefront property quickly?

Because it was liquid

Why did the accountant keep falling over?

She couldn't find her balance sheet

What do you do when a bull charges you?

You pay him!

Why was the accountant's self-esteem always so low?

Because he never gave himself enough "credit"

Why do cash analysts make great pirates?

Because they know a lot about treasury

How come the accountant never gave the asset any credit?

Because she didn't want to bring him down

What do you call the military officer in charge of accounting?

General Ledger

How come CFOs never use lowercase letters?

ABCDEFG

Because they're in charge of the "capital" structure

Where's the accountant's favorite place to shop?

The GAAP

Why was the expense late to the party?

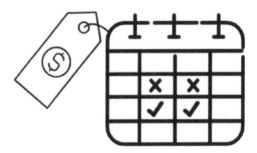

He forgot to put it on his fiscal schedule

How does a bird deposit their checks?

They go to the nearest branch

What do you call an "inventory" of boats?

Finished goods available for sail

Did you hear about the creditor who got bored?

He lost interest

What do you call a liability without any friends?

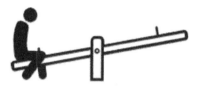

A loan

What do you call it when a group of executives falls back during battle?

A corporate retreat

How does a pig support his family?

He brings home the bacon

Why did the clean freak hate dealing with Cost of Goods Sold?

Because it always made their profit "gross"

P & L went to make an announcement...

Well I guess it was less of an announcement and more of an income statement

Why did the clown business go bankrupt after 5 years?

They had a large balloon loan

What kind of costs does a dishes company have?

They vary a bowl (variable)

What do you call a marathon for Accounts Payable Analysts?

A settlement run

How did the swimmers start an investment fund?

They pooled their money together

I just invested in a bakery...

It's supposed to have a great RO-Pie

My company keeps overspending trying to move this giant rock...

In other words, they can't budget

What does a volcano go into when it can't pay its mortgage?

Bankruption

What kind of bedding does an accountant have?

Balance Sheets

Why did the businessman throw all his money in the river?

He wanted to see his cash flow

Why was the banker bad at playing music?

Because they only knew how to play a Treasury note

I had to take out a loan for my lawn equipment...

It has a great Annual Percentage Rake

Did you hear about the frog who had $50,000 in debt?

He toad a lot of money

Why couldn't they sell the Tower of Pisa?

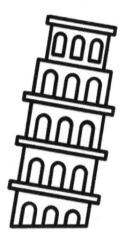

There was a "lien" on it

What type of credit line does the door company have?

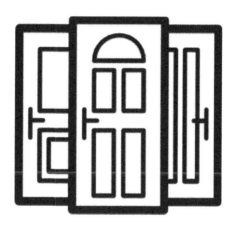

Revolving

How do you tell an accountant to be quiet?

You tell them to use their invoice

What did the revenue fish say to the expense fish?

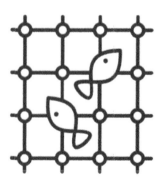

"Net incoming!"

What's it called when a Mastercard kicks a field goal?

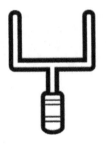

Credit score!

How did the mortgage on the deserted island feel?

A loan

Did you hear about all the shared expenses going to Hawaii?

It was their allo-cation

What do you call a vendor that never tells the truth?

A Supp-liar

What do you call dogs trying to establish an LLC?

Creating their "beagle" structure

How do you tell how profitable a butter company is?

Look at the "net margarine"

Why was the fishing store so valuable?

It had a lot of "net" worth

What do you call it when Quickbooks enters the atmosphere?

Journal Entry

Did you hear about the well-funded alphabet company?

They had 26 sources of "capital"

Why should you buy stock in the boulder company?

Because it's a rock solid investment!

Did you hear about the accountant who threw a dictionary on the grill?

She was trying to cook the books

What's an investor's favorite religion?

The one with the most prophets

Why are weather stations so bad at budgeting?

Because they can only do a 10-day forecast

My accounting friend is so mean…

She always laughs at my expense

Why do investors always buy Altoids?

They're great invest-mints!

What kind of spices does an accountant put on their steak?

Tax season-ing

Why did the cowboy walk into the financial advisor's office?

He was told it was a bull market

Why did Grizzly Adams walk into the financial advisor's office?

He was told it was a bear market

Where's an accountant's favorite place to hike?

The audit trail

What do farmers and accountants have in common?

They both spread-sheet

You made it to the end of the book!

You   Me

If you have enjoyed (most of) my jokes, then a review would be greatly appreciated!

If you're feeling generous you can go to www.amazon.com, search for "Extraordinary Dad Jokes", click this book in the search results, scroll down to the Reviews section, and click the "Write a customer review" button.

Thank you so much for reading. I hope you had a great time!